# From This Moment On
## & Other Great Love Songs

Project Manager: *Carol Cuellar*
Art Design: *Jorge Paredes*

# CONTENTS

# FROM THIS MOMENT ON

Words and Music by
SHANIA TWAIN and R.J. LANGE

From This Moment On - 7 - 1

4

6

# ALL MY LIFE

Words and Music by
RORY BENNETT and
JO JO HAILEY

All My Life - 7 - 1

*Bridge:*

all that_ I ev - er know;_ when you smile_ on my face,_ all I see_ is a glow._ You turn_

____ my life_ a - round,_ you pick_ me up____ when I____ was down._ You're

all that I ev - er know; when you smile, my face glow. You pick me up when I was down. Say, you

all that I ev - er know; when you smile, my face glow. You pick me up when I was down. And I

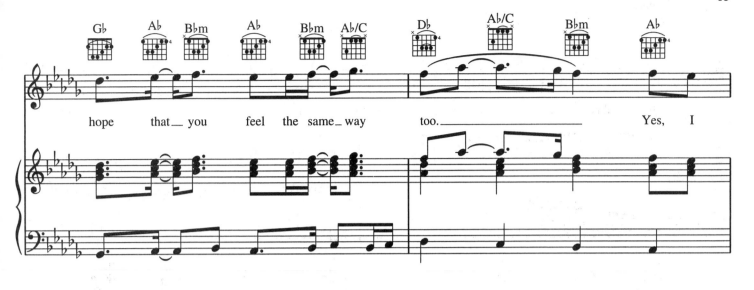

hope that you feel the same way too. Yes, I

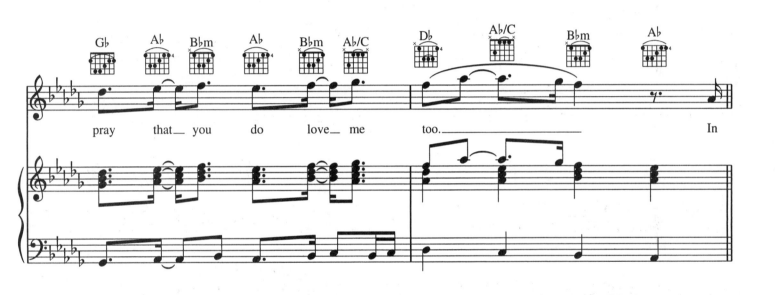

pray that you do love me too. In

*Chorus:*

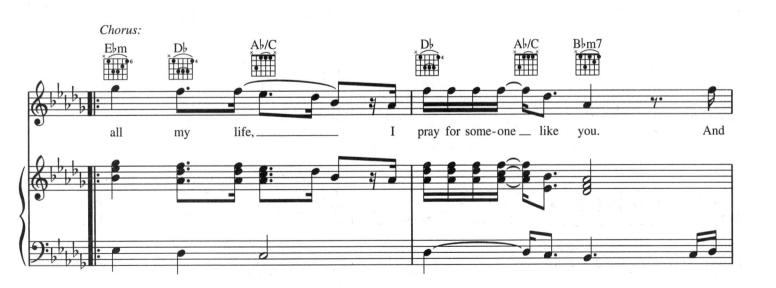

all my life, I pray for some-one like you. And

16

*Verse 2:*
Say, and I promise to never fall in love with a stranger.
You're all I'm thinkin', love, I praise the Lord above
For sendin' me your love, I cherish every hug.
I really love you so much.
*(To Chorus:)*

# BECAUSE YOU LOVED ME
## (Theme from "Up Close & Personal")

Words and Music by
DIANE WARREN

Because You Loved Me - 5 - 1

# BUTTERFLY KISSES

Words and Music by
BOB CARLISLE and RANDY THOMAS

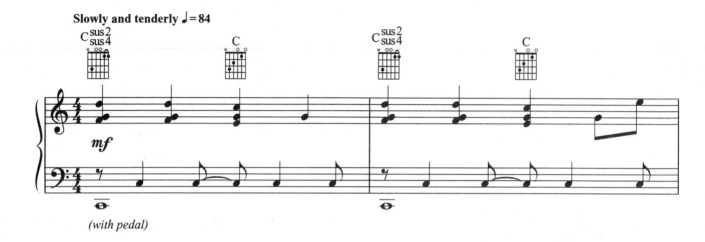

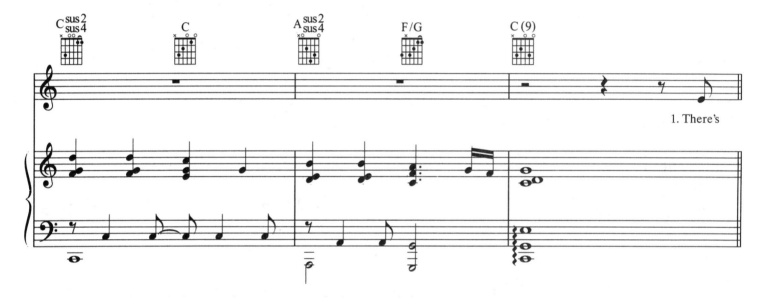

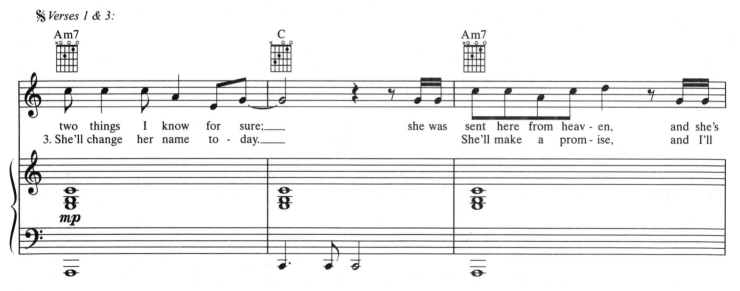

Butterfly Kisses - 7 - 1

28

love ev-'ry morn - ing and but-ter-fly kiss-es.__ I could-n't ask God__ for more,__ man,

this is what love is.____ I know I've got__ to let__ her go, but I'll al - ways____ re-mem-ber__

ev-'ry hug in the morn - ing and but-ter-fly kiss - es.____

# YOU MEAN THE WORLD TO ME

Words and Music by
L.A. REID, DARYL SIMMONS
and BABYFACE

You could
give me one good rea - son     why I should be - lieve___ you,     be -
gon - na take some work - ing,     but I be - lieve I'm worth it,     as

You Mean the World to Me - 5 - 3

33

You Mean the World to Me - 5 - 5

**From the Motion Picture "THE PREACHER'S WIFE"**

# I BELIEVE IN YOU AND ME

Words and Music by
SANDY LINZER and DAVID WOLFERT

*Verse 2:*
I will never leave your side,
I will never hurt your pride.
When all the chips are down,
I will always be around,
Just to be right where you are, my love.
Oh, I love you, boy.
I will never leave you out,
I will always let you in
To places no one has ever been.
Deep inside, can't you see?
I believe in you and me.
*(To Bridge:)*

*From the Motion Picture "THE MIRROR HAS TWO FACES"*

# I FINALLY FOUND SOMEONE

Words and Music by
BARBRA STREISAND, MARVIN HAMLISCH,
R.J. LANGE and BRYAN ADAMS

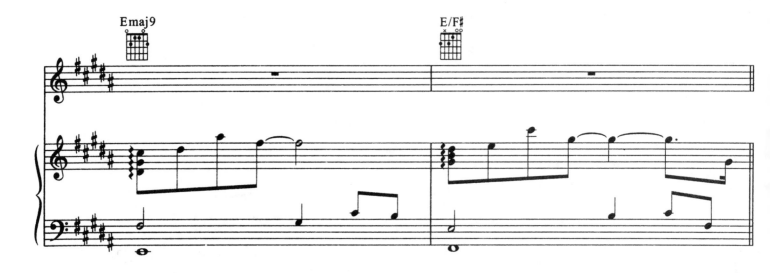

I Finally Found Someone - 8 - 1

I Finally Found Someone - 8 - 2

40

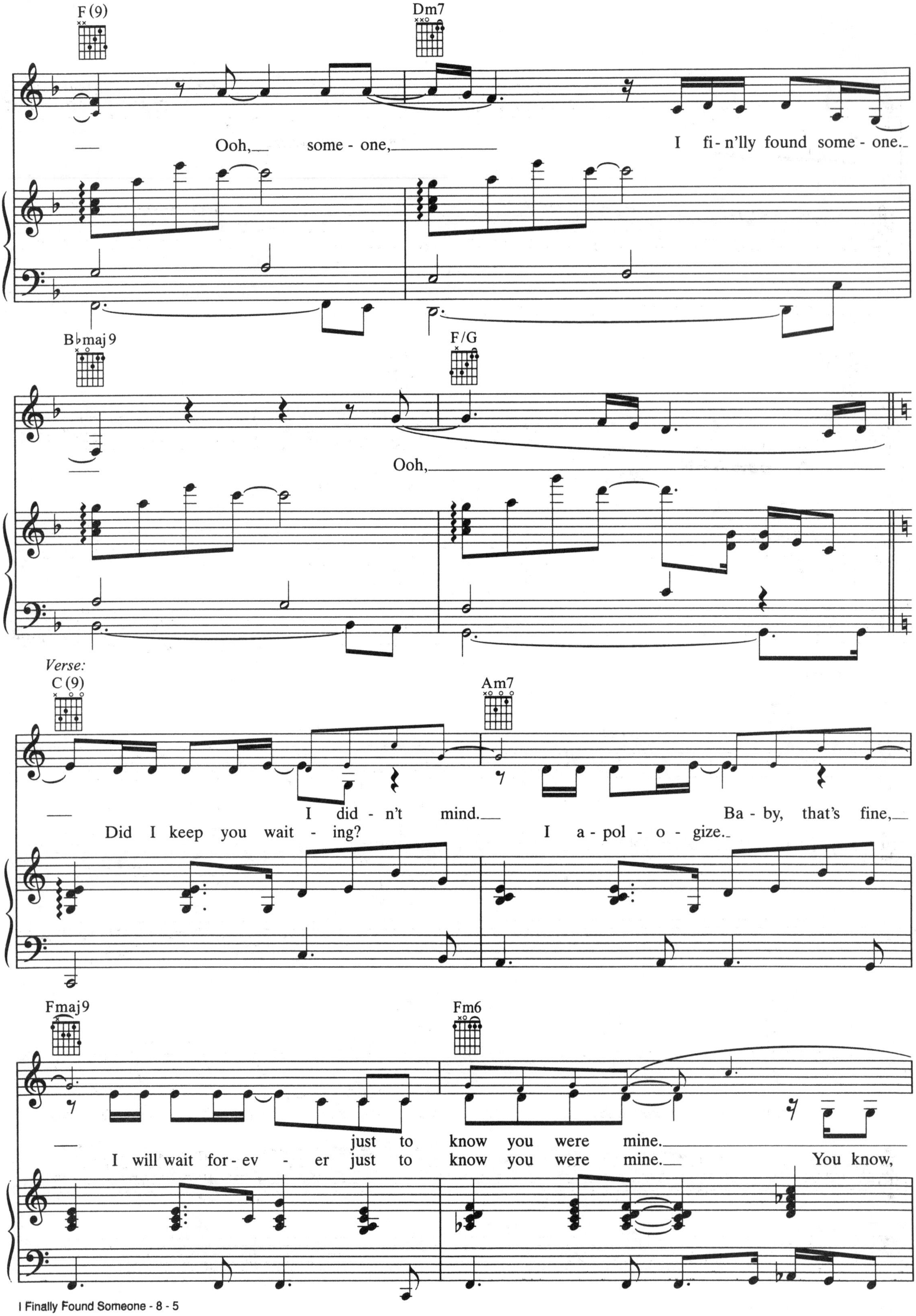

# I WILL COME TO YOU

Words and Music by
ISAAC HANSON, TAYLOR HANSON,
ZACHARY HANSON, BARRY MANN
and CYNTHIA WEIL

I Will Come to You - 6 - 1

# MY HEART WILL GO ON
## (Love Theme from "Titanic")

Words by
WILL JENNINGS

Music by
JAMES HORNER

My Heart Will Go On - 10 - 2

# OH HOW THE YEARS GO BY

Words and Music by
WILL JENNINGS and SIMON CLIMIE

64

Oh How the Years Go By - 6 - 3

Verse 2:
There were times we stumbled,
They thought they had us down,
We came around.
How we rolled and rambled,
We got lost and we got found.
Now we're back on solid ground.
We took everything
All our times would bring
In this world of danger.
'Cause when your heart is strong,
You know you're not alone
In this world of strangers.
(To Chorus:)

# VALENTINE

Composed by
JIM BRICKMAN and JACK KUGELL

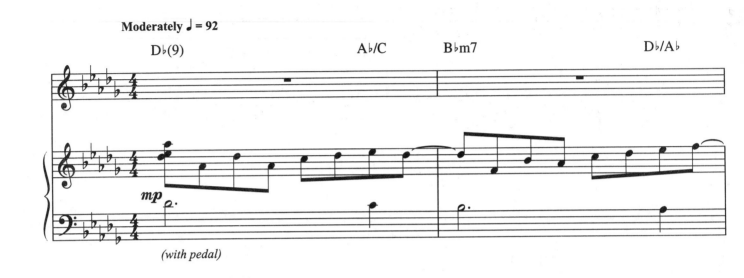

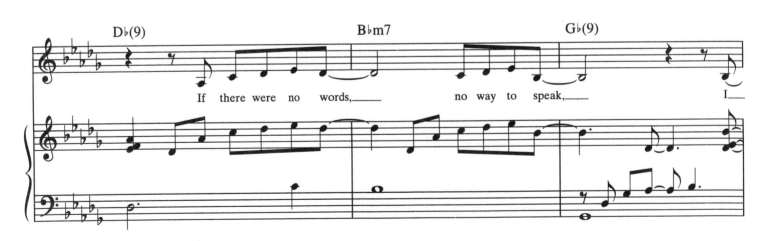

If there were no words,___ no way to speak,___ I

Valentine - 6 - 1

70

Valentine - 6 - 3

Valentine - 6 - 6

# SOMETHING ABOUT THE WAY
# YOU LOOK TONIGHT

Lyrics by
BERNIE TAUPIN

Music by
ELTON JOHN

Something About the Way You Look Tonight - 4 - 1

# TELL HIM

Words and Music by
LINDA THOMPSON, DAVID FOSTER
and WALTER AFANASIEFF

82

Tell Him - 6 - 5

Verse 2:
(Barbra:)
Touch him with the gentleness you feel inside. (C: I feel it.)
Your love can't be denied.
The truth will set you free.
You'll have what's meant to be.
All in time, you'll see.
(Celine:)
I love him, (B: Then show him.)
Of that much I can be sure. (B: Hold him close to you.)
I don't think I could endure
If I let him walk away
When I have so much to say.
(To Chorus:)

# KAREN'S THEME

Composed by
RICHARD CARPENTER

Karen's Theme - 3 - 1

# SOMETHING THAT WE DO

Guitar originally recorded
in alternate tuning (open D)
w/capo at 5th fret:

⑥ = D ③ = F#
⑤ = A ② = A
④ = D ① = D

Words and Music by
CLINT BLACK and SKIP EWING

Smoothly ♩ = 66

G     C     G

*mf*

*(with pedal)*

C     G     Am7     Am7/D     G

1. I re-

*Verses 1 & 2:*

D/G     C(9)     G

mem- ber well the day___ we wed,___ I can see that pic - ture in___ my head.___
2. *See additional lyrics*

C(9)     G     Am7     D

I still be-lieve the words___ we said___ for-ev- er will___ ring true.___

Something That We Do - 5 - 1

Something That We Do - 5 - 3

Verse 2:
It's holding tight, lettin' go,
It's flyin' high and layin' low.
Let your strongest feelings show
And your weakness, too.
It's a little and a lot to ask,
An endless and a welcome task.
Love isn't something that we have,
It's something that we do.
(To Bridge:)

# YOU WERE MEANT FOR ME

Moderate swing feel ♩ = 108

Words and Music by
JEWEL KILCHER and STEVE POLTZ

You Were Meant for Me - 5 - 1

**Verse 2:**
I called my mama, she was out for a walk.
Consoled a cup of coffee, but it didn't wanna talk.
So I picked up a paper, it was more bad news,
More hearts being broken or people being used.
Put on my coat in the pouring rain.
I saw a movie, it just wasn't the same,
'Cause it was happy and I was sad,
And it made me miss you, oh, so bad.
*(To Chorus:)*

**Verse 3:**
I brush my teeth and put the cap back on,
I know you hate it when I leave the light on.
I pick a book up and then I turn the sheets down,
And then I take a breath and a good look around.
Put on my pj's and hop into bed.
I'm half alive but I feel mostly dead.
I try and tell myself it'll be all right,
I just shouldn't think anymore tonight.
*(To Chorus:)*

# YOU'RE STILL THE ONE

Words and Music by
SHANIA TWAIN and R.J. LANGE

98

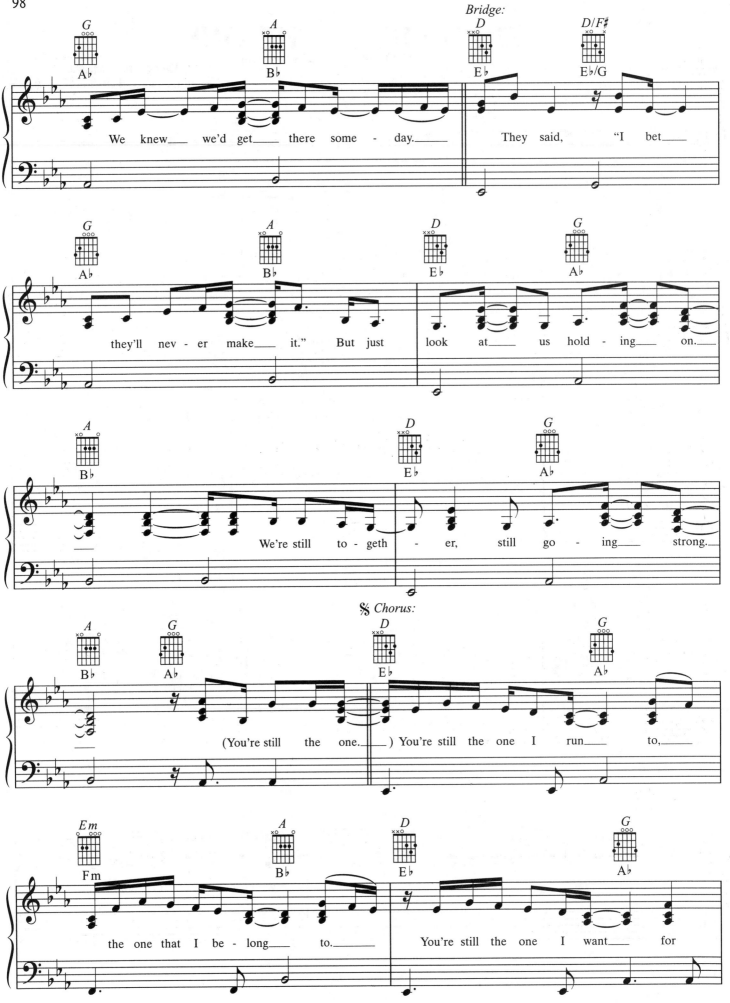

You're Still the One - 3 - 2

Verse 2:
Ain't nothin' better,
We beat the odds together.
I'm glad we didn't listen.
Look at what we would be missin'.
(To Bridge:)

You're Still the One - 3 - 3

# Showstoppers

## 100 or more titles in each volume of this Best-Selling Series!

**Piano/Vocal/Chords:**

### 20's, 30's, & 40's SHOWSTOPPERS
(F2865SMX)

100 nostalgic favorites include: Chattanooga Choo Choo ● Pennsylvania 6-5000 ● Blue Moon ● Moonglow ● My Blue Heaven ● Ain't Misbehavin' ● That Old Black Magic and more.

### 50's & 60's SHOWSTOPPERS
(F2864SMB)

Bop back to a simpler time and enjoy: Aquarius/Let the Sunshine In ● (Sittin' On) The Dock of the Bay ● Hey, Good Lookin' ● Sunny ● Johnny Angel and more.

### 70's & 80's SHOWSTOPPERS
P/V/C (F2863SME)
Easy Piano (F2863P2X)

100 pop songs from two decades. Titles include: Anything for You ● Blue Bayou ● Hungry Eyes ● I Wanna Dance with Somebody (Who Loves Me) ● If You Say My Eyes Are Beautiful ● I'll Never Love This Way Again ● Isn't She Lovely ● Old Time Rock & Roll ● When the Night Comes.

### BIG NOTE PIANO SHOWSTOPPERS
Vol. 1 (F2871P3C)   Vol. 2 (F2918P3A)

Easy-to-read big note arrangements of 100 popular tunes include: Do You Want to Know a Secret? ● If Ever You're in My Arms Again ● Moon River ● Over the Rainbow ● Singin' in the Rain ● You Light Up My Life ● Theme from *Love Story*.

### BROADWAY SHOWSTOPPERS
(F2878SMB)

100 great show tunes include: Ain't Misbehavin' ● Almost Like Being in Love ● Consider Yourself ● Give My Regards to Broadway ● Good Morning Starshine ● Mood Indigo ● Send in the Clowns ● Tomorrow.

### CHRISTMAS SHOWSTOPPERS
P/V/C (F2868SMA)
Easy Piano (F2924P2X)
Big Note (F2925P3X)

100 favorite holiday songs including: Sleigh Ride ● Silver Bells ● Deck the Halls ● Have Yourself a Merry Little Christmas ● Here Comes Santa Claus ● Little Drummer Boy ● Let It Snow! Let It Snow! Let It Snow!

### CLASSICAL PIANO SHOWSTOPPERS
(F2872P9X)

100 classical intermediate piano solos include: Arioso ● Bridal Chorus (from *Lohengrin*) ● Clair de Lune ● Fifth Symphony (Theme) ● Minuet in G ● Moonlight Sonata (1st Movement) ● Polovetsian Dance (from *Prince Igor*) ● The Swan ● Wedding March (from *A Midsummer Night's Dream*).

### COUNTRY SHOWSTOPPERS
(F2902SMC)

A fine collection of 101 favorite country classics and standards including: Cold, Cold Heart ● For the Good Times ● I'm So Lonesome I Could Cry ● There's a Tear in My Beer ● Young Country and more.

### EASY GUITAR SHOWSTOPPERS
(F2934EGA)

100 guitar arrangements of new chart hits, old favorites, classics and solid gold songs. Includes melody, chords and lyrics for songs like: Didn't We ● Love Theme from *St. Elmo's Fire* (For Just a Moment) ● Out Here on My Own ● Please Mr. Postman ● Proud Mary ● The Way He Makes Me Feel ● With You I'm Born Again ● You're the Inspiration.

### EASY LISTENING SHOWSTOPPERS
(F3069SMX)

85 easy listening songs including popular favorites, standards, TV and movie selections like: After All (Love Theme from *Chances Are)* ● From a Distance ● The Greatest Love of All ● Here We Are ● Theme from *Ice Castles* (Through the Eyes of Love) ● The Vows Go Unbroken (Always True to You) ● You Are So Beautiful.

### EASY ORGAN SHOWSTOPPERS
(F2873EOB)

100 great current hits and timeless standards in easy arrangements for organ include: After the Lovin' ● Always and Forever ● Come Saturday Morning ● I Just Called to Say I Love You ● Isn't She Lovely ● On the Wings of Love ● Up Where We Belong ● You Light Up My Life.

### EASY PIANO SHOWSTOPPERS
Vol. 1 (F2875P2D)   Vol. 2 (F2912P2C)

100 easy piano arrangements of familiar songs include: Alfie ● Baby Elephant Walk ● Classical Gas ● Don't Cry Out Loud ● Colour My World ● The Pink Panther ● I Honestly Love You.

### JAZZ SHOWSTOPPERS
(F2953SMX)

101 standard jazz tunes including: Misty ● Elmer's Tune ● Birth of the Blues ● It Don't Mean a Thing (If It Ain't Got That Swing).

### MOVIE SHOWSTOPPERS
(F2866SMC)

100 songs from memorable motion pictures include: Axel F ● Up Where We Belong ● Speak Softly Love (from *The Godfather)* ● The Entertainer ● Fame ● Nine to Five ● Nobody Does It Better.

### POPULAR PIANO SHOWSTOPPERS
(F2876P9B)

100 popular intermediate piano solos include: Baby Elephant Walk ● Gonna Fly Now (Theme from *Rocky)* ● The Hill Street Blues Theme ● Love Is a Many-Splendored Thing ● (Love Theme from) *Romeo and Juliet* ● Separate Lives (Love Theme from *White Nights)* ● The Shadow of Your Smile ● Theme from *The Apartment* ● Theme from *New York, New York*.

### RAGTIME SHOWSTOPPERS
(F2867SMX)

These 100 original classic rags by Scott Joplin, James Scott, Joseph Lamb and other ragtime composers include: Maple Leaf Rag ● The Entertainer ● Kansas City Rag ● Ma Rag Time Baby ● The St. Louis Rag ● World's Fair Rag and many others.

### ROMANTIC SHOWSTOPPERS
(F2870SMC)

101 beautiful songs including: After All (Love Theme from *Chances Are)* ● Here and Now ● I Can't Stop Loving You ● If You Say My Eyes Are Beautiful ● The Vows Go Unbroken (Always True to You) ● You Got It.

### TELEVISION SHOWSTOPPERS
(F2874SMC)

103 TV themes including: Another World ● Dear John ● Hall or Nothing (The Arsenio Hall Show) ● Star Trek -The Next Generation (Main Title) ● Theme from "Cheers" (Where Everybody Knows Your Name).